BIBLE TOOLKIT

A New Believer's Guide to the Bible

Christopher J. Weeks

THE FIRST PLACE TO START

CONTENTS

Many people are afraid to admit that the Bible is very intimidating, confusing, and hard to understand. Some new believers have tried to begin a New Year's resolution to study the Bible only to find themselves quitting after a few weeks from frustration and even boredom.

If the Bible seems intimidating and overwhelming to you, this guide it written with you in mind. Hopefully the helps that are found in this booklet will take away some of the fear and trepidation of opening and exploring the untold riches found in God's Word.

Think of this booklet as your own personal tour guide of the Bible. Learn how to. . .

- ◆ **Read the Old and New Testaments**
- ◆ **Identify the purpose of each book**
- ◆ **Find chapters and verses**
- ◆ **Study to gain insight for yourself**

This booklet is just a start. It gives you the basics and hopefully it will serve as a great resource as you continue to grow in your study habits.

❖ *"Now what I am commanding you today is not too difficult for you or beyond your reach...No, the word is very near you." —**Deuteronomy 30:11 & 14***

The words are familiar, but what do they mean? Bible, Testament, Prophet and Psalms? Remember, what may seem obvious to everyone but you is usually obvious to none. So, to get a proper hold of the Bible we will start with some simple definitions to help you learn the "Christian lingo" without feeling left out. Let us start as easy as we can:

BIBLE: Originally it has its root in the word paper, binding and book. For the general public of today, it refers to the collection of writings that contain the Jewish and Christian scriptures; or those books and letters which are considered by people of faith to be from God himself.

TESTAMENT: This word means a couple of things in the Biblical narrative:

a. An agreement between God and man; if man believes what God says, blessings will come.

b. A set of laws and documents that are ratified by the death of some person or animal.

OLD TESTAMENT: The writings that were originally given God's people, the Jews. It begins at creation and ends at the prophet Malachi, 400 years before Jesus' birth. It was later recognized by the Christians as the historical and theological foundation for the ministry of Christ.

NEW TESTAMENT: The writings that were given to all of God's people, the Christians. It begins at Jesus' birth and ends at the book of Revelation which discusses the "End of All Things."

GOSPEL: This is a word that simply means, "Good News." In the structure of the Biblical books, it means an eyewitness account of the life of Jesus Christ and his ministry.

EPISTLE: The word simply means a "letter." The epistles are written by certain followers of Jesus to the churches in the towns the letter is written to.

PROPHET: This is a man who was sent from God to speak the words of God to men.

APOSTLE: This is a man who was sent from Jesus to speak the words of Jesus to men. They are the original 12 disciples (followers) of Jesus, and also Paul who took Judas' place.

CHURCH: A group of people who are assembled together to worship Jesus Christ as God. They meet to learn from the Bible, pray together, encourage each other and help bring new people outside of the church to believe in Jesus as well.

PRIEST: A person who brings sacrifices to God on behalf of men.

THE LAW OF MOSES: The 10 commandments and other laws that Moses brought down from Mt. Sinai to give as a guideline for God's people, the Jews, to follow.

THE TRINITY: The Christian's belief that God is three persons in one Godhead. The three persons include:

- God the Father: He who is the great "I Am"
- God the Son: Jesus Christ of Nazareth
- God the Holy Spirit: The Spirit who lives in believers

SALVATION: The means by which we are brought into a right relationship with God, and we have a secure future in his presence forever.

FINDING AN ADDRESS

Before we familiarize ourselves with the whole structure of the Bible itself, let us learn one simple little task that will help us: FINDING AN ADDRESS of a Bible verse. Often you will hear someone say, "I love this verse, John 3:16." To avoid embarrassment, many people will act like they know what John 3:16 is but they don't really understand what the name and numbers stand for. So let's take a look:

JOHN 3 : 16

You will find the books in the table of contents at the beginning of your bible and they will have a page number to tell you where in the bible to turn, that is the easiest way to begin.

What does John 3:16 say?

_____

_____

_____

Now try to find these addresses:

1. Genesis 1:1

_____

_____

2. Psalm 23:5

_____

_____

3. 2 Timothy 3:14-16

_____

_____

_____

Are you finding it easy to look up the books and addresses? Keep trying, it will become easy.

A LOOK AT THE BOOKS

A LOOK AT THE BOOKS

Ah, it is time to open up that book called the Bible and get familiar with it. The easiest way to do this is simply turning to the very front and look for "A Table of Contents." Look at how the bible is arranged:

1. The Two Sections: Old and New Testaments

2. The List of Books in Each Testament

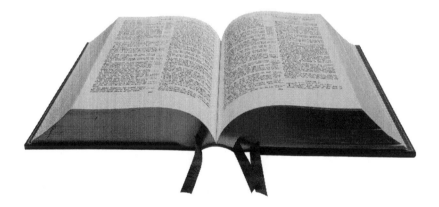

We will examine those two areas and walk you through them.

THE OLD TESTAMENT

As we have already defined, the Old Testament is simply a list of writings that are given to God's people, the Jews, through inspired writers. When I say inspired, I mean people who God chose to use to carry his very words through their specific personalities and historical circumstances. For instance, the book of "Amos" was a book written by Amos who was a farmer, and God sent him to tell people to wake up and start living right. Very simple! In the Old Testament, there are 39 books that have been historically accepted by all Christians as God's true words.

▶ THE LIST OF BOOKS IN THE OLD TESTAMENT:

Let us look each of the books that are listed under the Old Testament by looking at 3 things: The Author, the date of writing, and why it was written. This will give you a good grasp on why the book was written.

GENESIS: Author: Moses | Date: 1450-1410B.C.

Purpose of Book: A Book of Beginnings: The World, Man, Sin, the Nations and God's people called Israel.

EXODUS: Author: Moses | Date: 1450-1410 B.C.

Purpose of Book: Deliverance of God's people from the captivity of the Egyptians by the person of Moses.

LEVITICUS: Author: Moses | Date: 1410 B.C.

Purpose of Book: How to have Holiness before God through the Law.

NUMBERS: Author: Moses | Date: 1410 B.C.

Purpose of Book: Transition book from deliverance from Egypt to wanderings in the desert before the promised land of Canaan. Lessons on trusting God and sins of unbelief.

DEUTERONOMY: Author: Moses | Date: 1410 B.C.

Purpose of Book: It is the second giving of the Law, and it can be looked at as Israel's Constitution and treaty with God.

JOSHUA: Author: Joshua | Date: 1100-1370B.C.

Purpose of Book: The conquest of the promised land by Joshua and Israel.

JUDGES: Author: Unknown | Date: 1050-1000 B.C.

Purpose of Book: A historical book about the time of the Judges, men who ruled but were not king. It was a time of disobedience to obedience and back again.

RUTH: Author: Uncertain | Date: 1000 B.C.

Purpose of Book: A historical book of the life of a non-Jew named Ruth who lived during the times of the judges and her marriage to Boaz who was a Jew.

1 SAMUEL: Author: Samuel and Others | Date: 930 B.C.

Purpose of Book: A book from the last judge to the establishment of kings: Saul and David.

2 SAMUEL: Author: Uncertain | Date: 930 B.C.

Purpose of Book: The reign of King David and the prominence of Jerusalem as the center of Jewish power.

I KINGS: Author: Jeremiah | Date: 550 B.C.

Purpose of Book: The successive reign of the Jewish Kings, highlighting blessing with obedience and curses with disobedience.

2 KINGS: Author: Jeremiah | Date: 550 B.C.

Purpose of Book: The continuation of the kings until they go into captivity from their disobedience to God.

I CHRONICLES: Author: Ezra | Date: 450-425 B.C.

Purpose of Book: The reign of the Kings from a priestly perspective. Starting once again with King David.

2 CHRONICLES: Author: Ezra | Date: 450-425 B.C.

Purpose of Book: The continuation of the kings until they go into captivity from their disobedience to God.

EZRA: Author: Ezra | Date: 456–444 B.C.

Purpose of Book: The fulfillment of God's promise to restore Israel to her land after the 70 years of captivity.

NEHEMIAH: Author: Nehemiah | Date: 445-425 B.C.

Purpose of Book: The completion of the return, restoration and rebuilding of the temple.

ESTHER: Author: Uncertain | Date: 465 B.C.

Purpose of Book: The story of Esther and her promotion to be the Queen of the Persians for the purpose of saving the Jewish race.

JOB: Author: Uncertain | Date: Uncertain

Purpose of Book: The issue of why righteous men suffer, through the experiences of Job.

PSALMS: Author: Various | Date: Various B.C.

Purpose of Book: A book of Hebrew poetry and songs that declare: God's greatness, beauty, and love; while dealing with man's fears, pain and joy.

PROVERBS: Author: Solomon & Others | Date: 950-700 B.C.

Purpose of Book: The sayings of wisdom for living. Instructions on folly, sin, wealth, words, love, lust, gluttony, and etc.

ECCLESIASTES: Author: Solomon | Date: 935 B.C.

Purpose of Book: A book of philosophy when looking at life through the perspective of secular man.

SONG OF SONGS: Author: Solomon | Date: 965 B.C.

Purpose of Book: A poem of love between Solomon and his first wife.

ISAIAH: Author: Isaiah | Date: 740 –680 B.C.

Purpose of Book: Isaiah's pleading to the nation of Israel to follow God.

JEREMIAH: Author: Jeremiah | Date: 627-585 B.C.

Purpose of Book: Warnings of judgment to Jerusalem because they failed to follow God.

LAMENTATIONS: Author: Jeremiah | Date: 586 B.C.

Purpose of Book: A book of poetic lamentations of sorrow as the prophet looks at the destruction of Jerusalem.

EZEKIEL: Author: Ezekiel | Date: 592-570 B.C.

Purpose of Book: God will keep his covenant even though your sins are ever before you.

DANIEL: Author: Daniel | Date: 537 B.C.

Purpose of Book: God's dealings with the nations of the world which includes major end times prophecies as well as historical events.

HOSEA: Author: Hosea | Date: 710 B.C.

Purpose of Book: God orders a prophet to marry a prostitute to show how God's people have committed infidelity towards God.

JOEL: Author: Joel | Date: 835 B.C.

Purpose of Book: The Day of the Lord is coming and it will be a great day as well as a day of utter devastation.

AMOS: Author: Amos | Date: 755 B.C.

Purpose of Book: Because of your evils against society and pagan worship, judgment is near and you need to turn back to God.

OBADIAH: Author: Obadiah | Date: 592-570 B.C.

Purpose of Book: Edom stands judged because of her pride for rejoicing over the fall of God's people.

JONAH: Author: Jonah | Date: 760 B.C.

Purpose of Book: Story of a man running from the will of God because he lacks compassion for the lost.

MICAH: Author: Micah | Date: 700 B.C.

Purpose of Book: Judgment is coming to God's people and we need to turn back to God back walking humbly, doing justice to others, and loving mercy.

NAHUM: Author: Nahum | Date: 663-612 B.C.

Purpose of Book: God is powerful, and nations like Nineveh who scorn God will be judged.

HABAKKUK: Author: Habakkuk | Date: 607 B.C.

Purpose of Book: Why does God not judge those who do evil? His mercy is extended but there will be a day of justice.

ZEPHANIAH: Author: Zephaniah | Date: 625 B.C.

Purpose of Book: Judgment is certain, but God's promises stand. The Day of the Lord will bring about the total destruction of the heathen nations.

HAGGAI: Author: Haggai | Date: 520 B.C.

Purpose of Book: A book to encourage people to rebuild God's broken house.

ZECHERIAH: Author: Ezekiel | Date: 520-518 B.C.

Purpose of Book: Consolation and hope because God will restore the fortunes of those who repent and look forward to the coming of the Messiah.

MALACHI: Author: Malachi | Date: 450-400 B.C.

Purpose of Book: A rebuke for neglecting true worship and call to repentance.

THE NEW TESTAMENT

As we have already defined, the New Testament is simply a list of writings that are given to all of God's people, the Christians, through inspired writers. In the New Testament, there are 27 books that have been historically accepted by all Christians as God's true words.

▶ THE LIST OF BOOKS IN THE NEW TESTAMENT:

Let us look each of the books that are listed under the New Testament by again looking at 3 things: The Author, the date of writing, and why it was written. This will give you a good grasp on why the book was written.

MATTHEW: Author: Matthew | Date: 60 A.D.

Purpose of Book: The life of Christ from the perspective of a Jew and how he fulfills all Old Testament scripture surrounding him to prove he is the Messiah.

MARK: Author: Mark | Date: 50A.D.

Purpose of Book: The life of Christ from the perspective of a disciple who wants the Roman world to know that he is the most powerful servant of God, ever.

LUKE: Author: Luke | Date: 60 A.D.

Purpose of Book: The life of Christ from the perspective of a Doctor who wants the Greek world to know that Jesus is the greatest man who ever lived.

JOHN: Author: John the apostle | Date: 85-90 A.D.

Purpose of Book: The life of Christ from the perspective of a man who wants everyone in the whole world to know that Jesus Christ is God.

ACTS: Author: Luke | Date: 61 A.D.

Purpose of Book: The beginning of the early church and the spread of the good news of Jesus through the apostles.

ROMANS: Author: Paul | Date: 58 A.D.

Purpose of Book: This is a look at what all of Christianity is in a nutshell: From being lost, to salvation by faith, to walking in the Spirit, and how you live in the church.

1 CORINTHIANS: Author: Paul | Date: 56 A.D.

Purpose of Book: This helps deal with problems in the church. From thinking some teachers are better than others, to sexual sin and the misuse of gifts.

2 CORINTHIANS: Author: Paul | Date: 57 A.D.

Purpose of Book: The second letter that Paul sent to the Corinthian church to warn them about false apostles and how he loves them with his whole heart.

GALATIANS: Author: Paul | Date: 49-55 A.D.

Purpose of Book: A letter written to people who are going back to following the Law of Moses after they came to Christ by faith, and Paul is warning them to live by faith not law.

EPHESIANS: Author: Paul | Date: 61 A.D.

Purpose of Book: This letter is about the whole purpose and design of the church body. It discusses how a person can fully be a part of God's plan for the church.

COLOSSIANS: Author: Paul | Date: 61 A.D.

Purpose of Book: This letter is about how Christ is to have supremacy above everything: including worldly philosophies and religions. And it discusses the importance of unity.

1 THESSALONIANS: Author: Paul | Date: 51 A.D.

Purpose of Book: This letter is about the coming of Christ in the last days and how we need to be diligently looking and working before he comes.

2 THESSALONIANS: Author: Paul | Date: 59 A.D.

Purpose of Book: This letter continues with the issues surrounding the last days including the anti-Christ and how we need to stay busy in our walk.

1 TIMOTHY: Author: Paul | Date: 63 A.D.

Purpose of Book: This is a letter of instruction for a young pastor on how to build a body of believers.

2 TIMOTHY: Author: Paul | Date: 66 A.D.

Purpose of Book: This letter is Paul's plea for Timothy to stay strong in the ministry and to watch out for the apostasy that will come as the end comes closer.

TITUS: Author: Paul | Date: 65 A.D.

Purpose of Book: This letter is instructions for Titus on how to teach a body of believers.

PHILEMON: Author: Paul | Date: 61 A.D.

Purpose of Book: Paul is writing on behalf of a runaway slave named Onesimus, and asking his previous owner to take him back and treat him as a brother in Christ.

HEBREWS: Author: Uncertain | Date 64-68 A.D.

Purpose of Book: This letter is written to Jewish Christians who are enduring amazing persecution and they are falling back to Mosaic law for comfort, and the writer says NO find your answers in Christ alone.

JAMES: Author: James, Jesus' brother | Date: 45-50 A.D.

Purpose of Book: This is a New Testament book of Proverbs on how to carry on in trials and to live a godly life.

1 PETER: Author: Peter | Date: 63 A.D.

Purpose of Book: This letter is about persevering under suffering and teaching how to live as a true follower of Christ.

2 PETER: Author: Peter | Date: 66 A.D.

Purpose of Book: This letter is to remind believers what he first taught and warning against false teachers.

1 JOHN: Author: John | Date: 90 A.D.

Purpose of Book: This letter is about having certainty that you are indeed a child of God, and it gives the tangible ways you can tell.

2 JOHN: Author: John | Date: 90 A.D.

Purpose of Book: This letter is a plea for Christians to continue walking in Christ commandments.

3 JOHN: Author: John | Date: 90 A.D.

Purpose of Book: This letter is a rebuke on a false teacher.

JUDE: Author: Jude, Jesus' brother | Date: 70-80 A.D.

Purpose of Book: This letter is for the purpose of condemning false teachers and encouraging the believers to keep contending for the faith as the days grow evil.

REVELATION: Author: John | Date: 90 A.D.

Purpose of Book: This letter concerns all the subjects that pertain to the end of the world and the future reign of Christ.

CANONICITY

▸ WHY THESES BOOKS?

One question that needs to be addressed is the question of Canonicity. In other words, why are these 66 books considered God's Word? Why not the writings of C.S. Lewis or the Koran? There is a test that church leaders through the ages have used and it is called the *Test of Canonicity*, which means the books that contain the standard or correct rulings of God. Three issues are considered:

- **Authority of the Writer:** A writer must either a prophet of God, disciple of Jesus Christ, or have had close personal contact with a disciple.

- **Biblically Consistent:** A book must not contradict obvious teachings and doctrines of other books and they must maintain the same themes of Redemption.

- **Church Recognized Its Truth:** The early church started recognizing different books as God's written word and they would make copies and pass around the books that were obviously sent from God. It is like a prospector who is looking for gold, they know it when they find it!

It is often said the early church determined the standard, as if God's Word was the invention of a few patriarchal and controlling men. But the early church, as well as subsequent Christians of every nation and tribe, simply recognized God's imprint and power on his words. They didn't create the Bible, they received it!

▸ WHY THE BIBLE PRACTICALLY MATTERS

All of us expect other people to speak to us in a way that makes sense. If you didn't, you would never read your emails, go on social media rants or even read your mom's handwritten notes in the first place.

Therefore, if human beings can adjust their language so ideas are transmitted with accuracy and clarity, don't you think God can exercise the same ability? Some post-modern scholars aren't too sure about this. They think God is so unlike us that He is unable to be properly understood. But I believe that since God made us, he knows exactly how to communicate with us! So when we are looking for meaning, purpose and clear explanations, I believe God has spoken and still speaks and is not playing a game of Hide-n-Go-Seek with us. In fact, He loves it when we seek the truth (Isaiah 55:6).

How does the writer in Psalm 19:1-9 describe the way God communicates with the world?

Scholars say that God speaks through two clear vehicles:

1. NATURE (verse 3): "There is no speech or language where their voice is not heard. Their voice goes out into all the earth." The beauty of the earth, the wonder of the heavens, the brilliant fine-tuning of the ecosystem displays the mind of a genius. Sure, people try to explain it away by random chance, but deep down in the gut of a human's soul, people know God did this. So why is there such a huge movement to push God out of public discourse, to mock Intelligent Design, to force a monolithic mind-meld concerning evolution? Simple: out of sight, out of mind. God's invisibility allows for the prideful man to believe his own lies about his delusion of "supposed" greatness. How does Romans 1:18-25 describe the attitude of the world toward God and his truth?

_____

_____

_____

_____

In other words, people know God exists, but they would rather ignore him so they suppress the truth he gave to us. That is why God communicated through...

2. HIS WORD (verse 7): "The law of the Lord is perfect, reviving the soul." God's Word is perfect in that it accurately represents reality, as it is. And it is perfect in the sense that it speaks to us on our level -- it is designed to be understood. Yes, God is Infinite, Holy and Transcendent (above us in every way), but He knows how we think because he made our brain. When a dad talks to his 2-year-old daughter does He use words like "existentialism", "sophistry" and "hermeneutics"? Of course not, he speaks in a language that perfectly connects with the mind of his daughter and they have a real relationship. In fact, sometimes it is easier to communicate with a 2-year-old as compared to an 18-year-old. So why don't people understand God's Word? Why does it seem so confusing? Here is my simple, non-highfalutin' reply: People don't want to communicate to Almighty God because they believe they have better things to do.

▶ GOD SPEAKS IN WAYS WE CAN UNDERSTAND

1. God's Word is intended **to be understood:** Luke 1:1-4 says what?

However, you must put forth some effort to understand it. Look at how 2 Timothy 2:15 describes what an authentic Christian does:

I don't buy it when people say the words are too big, the concept is too fuzzy or it's too confusing. Just ask them questions in their area of interest; Computer geeks use big words like Gigabyte, Active-Matrix and Hexadecimal. Social savvy teens have their own language such as BTW, CUL8R and FOCL. Brainless football fans use terms like Line of Scrimmage, Intentional Grounding, 2 Gap 3-4 Defensive Schemes. To find gold you must dig.

2. God's Word is never presented as a fairy tale, it is **meant to be read seriously:** 2 Peter 1:16 says what?

1 John 1:1-3 also talks about the God's Word:

John saw Jesus with his very own eyes. He heard Jesus, touched Jesus, and saw Jesus. What do you think that would be like?

The Old Testament writers often didn't want to speak but they had to. Look at what the Prophet Jeremiah says in Jeremiah 20:7-9:

Proper communication must respect the intent of the person speaking. If I told you something serious like my dad died and you said that I was "speaking in a vague poetic genre that was open to a wide variety of interpretations dependent on the cultural community of the time of my utterance" I would punch you right in the nose. The reason I would punch you is that you were purposely not trying to understand me!

3. Finally, and this must be heard, **God's Word is dangerous;** don't play around with it. Put 2 Peter 3:16 in your own words:

So, if you purposely distort its meaning you will be destroyed. Look how Proverbs 30:6 confirms this:

God will defend its trustworthiness. Maybe one of the most terrifying verses in all of scripture is found in Revelation 22:18-19. What does it say?

It isn't complicated. The decay in society, destruction of families, explosion of perversity, moral and intellectual ruin, even poverty all begins with the "lack of delight in God's Word." If you don't believe me, listen to Jeremiah 6:10. What does he say?

I want to close with a perfect example of how, when left alone to our own devices, humans use language to complicate things, not make them clear. Almost every day we hear about a celebrity couple getting a divorce after only a few years of marriage. Scripture is very clear on its warning, "God hates divorce" (Malachi 2:16). But no, not in our sophisticated day and age; divorce is a much more complex issue. Listen to this article from Dr. Habib Sadeghi and Dr. Sherry Sami: "When the whole concept of marriage and divorce is reexamined, there's actually something far more powerful—and positive— at play." The doctors consider how insects might be able to tell us something about divorce. They continue:

"The misunderstandings involved in divorce also have much to do with the lack of intercourse between our own internal masculine and feminine energies. Choosing to hide within an endoskeleton and remain in attack mode requires a great imbalance of masculine energy. Feminine energy is the source of peacemaking, nurturing, and healing. Cultivating your feminine energy during this time is beneficial to the success of conscious uncoupling. When our masculine and feminine energies reach equilibrium once more, we can emerge from our old relationship and consciously call in someone who reflects our new world, not the old one."

So you tell me, who is easier to understand, God or our "enlightened" experts?

SPECIFIC STUDIES

FOR NEW BELIEVERS

Hopefully you have already read through the companion book, "New Believers: A Four-Week Study Guide", and have learned some basic ways to begin approaching the Bible. For review we discussed some of the possible avenues you can take to understand God's written communication to us:

▶ A WORD STUDY: This is studying a specific word that you have had some questions and confusion about. I have listed some suggestions to get you started so you can get familiar with your Bible.

♦ **Verses on Faith:**

Hebrews 11:1-6:

Romans 10:17:

Romans 5:1:

Galatians 2:15-21:

- **Verses on Hope:**

Romans 8:22-25:

Hebrews 6:13-19:

Romans 5:2-5:

Titus 2:13:

- **Verses on Love:**

1 Corinthians 13:1-13:

Romans 12:9-10:

1 Timothy 1:5:

1 John 4:7-21:

▶ A TOPICAL STUDY: This is studying a whole are that you are interested in. A person, place or concept. Here are some important topics and questions related to the topic and places to find some of the answers.

- **The Church:**

How did the first church come about? Read Acts 2. Write down what you find:

_____

_____

_____

_____

_____

Why does the church mean so much to God?" Read Ephesians 2:20-3:12 to find the answer:

_____

_____

_____

_____

_____

- **The Holy Spirit:**

Who is the Holy Spirit and what is his purpose? Read John 14:15-27 & 16:4-15 and write all that the Spirit will do when he comes:

_____

_____

_____

_____

How can a person know if the Holy Spirit is alive in their life? Read Galatians 5:16-23 & 1 John 2:20-27 and describe characteristics that reveal when the Spirit of God is working in a person's life:

_____

_____

_____

_____

_____

- **Spiritual Warfare:**

Who is the Devil and why should we be worried about him? Read 1 Peter 5:6-9 & 2 Timothy 2:22-26 and describe what you have found:

_____

_____

_____

How are we supposed to fight an entity we cannot see? Read 2 Corinthians 10:3-6 & Ephesians 6:10-18 and detail what we are up against:

_____

_____

_____

_____

_____

MAKE IT YOUR GOAL TO PLEASE HIM!

▸ A BOOK STUDY: This is studying a whole book in the bible that you would like to know well.

If you need help in how to grow in depth in these areas ask the person you're studying the Bible with, which one has helped them. But remember, study the bible in the way that is the most HELPFUL for you to grow. But what I have found most helpful to really make the Bible my own is knowing three things:

1. Seeing how the different books in the Bible fit with real History

2. Seeing who the Bible is all about.

3. Learning how I apply it to my life.

The Bible has been given to us to grow in Christ. What does Romans 10:17 say?

So if you want to mature, you must learn to use the Bible. Sadly, many believers stop reading thinking they have arrived. How does the writer to Hebrews 5:11-6:4?

THE BIBLE & HISTORY

There are hundreds if not thousands of Bible helps on-line to give people visual aids in seeing how the Bible is put together. But I want to give you some terms and different timelines that will serve as a quick reference guide for you to use as an aid in your study as you try to make sense of the wide scope of scripture.

▶ THE PATRIARCHAL PERIOD

This is the period of history where everything began. A Patriarch is a "Father of Faith." The Patriarchal Period starts with Adam, the first human, and includes Noah, Abraham, Isaac, Jacob and Joseph. In this period God began the story of redemption: "saving mankind from his sin in order to restore him back to his original created design." So in this period, you have creation, where God made man and gave him the mandate to "fill and subdue the earth" and then sin entered the world through Adam's sin. As a result of sin and its damaging effects on the created order, God brought on the flood and separated the nations at Babel. So to bring humanity back to himself, he chose a specific tribe of people out of the world, the Hebrews, to form a relationship of love with him called a "covenant." Abraham was the first "Father of Faith" that he called and then his sons continued on in the covenant promises that were first given to Abraham. Here is a general idea of the timeline and where you can find the written accounts.

THE PATRIARCHAL PERIOD

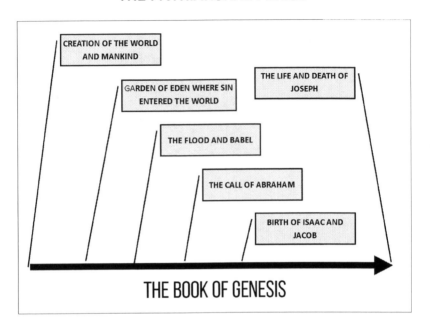

CREATION OF THE WORLD AND MANKIND

GARDEN OF EDEN WHERE SIN ENTERED THE WORLD

THE LIFE AND DEATH OF JOSEPH

THE FLOOD AND BABEL

THE CALL OF ABRAHAM

BIRTH OF ISAAC AND JACOB

THE BOOK OF GENESIS

▶ THE EXODUS AND WANDERING

This is the period of history where the prophet Moses was called by God to lead his people out of Egypt where they were being used as slaves for over 400 years. After God rescued them from the hand of Pharaoh (Egyptian King) they wandered for 40 years in the desert of Sinai. It was there God gave them the Law and prepared them to enter the Promised Land.

THE EXODUS AND WANDERING

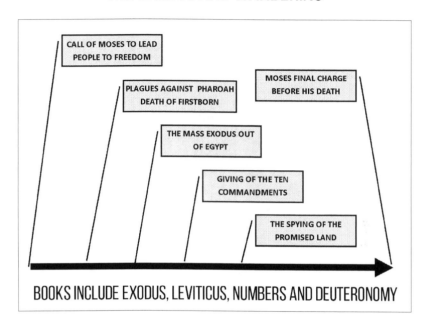

CALL OF MOSES TO LEAD PEOPLE TO FREEDOM

MOSES FINAL CHARGE BEFORE HIS DEATH

PLAGUES AGAINST PHAROAH DEATH OF FIRSTBORN

THE MASS EXODUS OUT OF EGYPT

GIVING OF THE TEN COMMANDMENTS

THE SPYING OF THE PROMISED LAND

BOOKS INCLUDE EXODUS, LEVITICUS, NUMBERS AND DEUTERONOMY

▶ THE JUDGES TO THE REIGN OF KING DAVID

This is the period of history where God's people, the Hebrews, also known as the Jews and Israel, entered the promised land of Canaan. It was during this time where God commanded the Jews to conquer the land and take it over to set up a Jewish nation-state built on his rule, a Theocracy. Over the years the Jews would follow a similar downward spiral of disobedience, bondage to the ungodly Canaanite nations, despair and then being rescued by a Judge that God sent. After many years of following this same destructive pattern, the Jews demanded from God to have their own king who would build for them a powerful nation, stopping this cycle. The first King "anointed" by God was Saul, an arrogant and selfish man, and then he chooses King David to take his throne, who was "a man after God's own heart." Through King David, he eventually brought great fame and prosperity for the nation Israel.

THE JUDGES TO THE REIGN OF KING DAVID

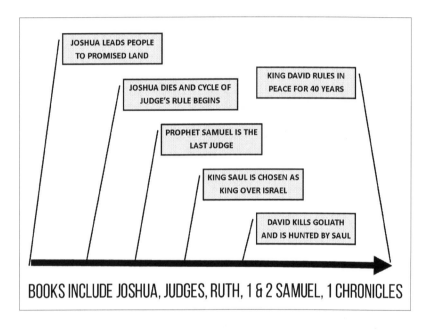

SOLOMON TO SLAVERY

This is the period of history where Israel was ruled by a series of disobedient Kings. Starting with Solomon, who ruled over a peaceful Israel because of the promises given to his father David; Solomon began another pattern of disobedience which eventually led to the nation of Israel going into captivity. During this time, the nation Israel was split into two factions:

The Northern Kingdom called Israel, and the Southern Kingdom called Judah. Israel's kings of the north allowed for the worship of other gods provoking God to anger. Eventually, they were invaded by the nation Assyria and were dragged away into captivity. Judah's kings to the south had a closer walk with God, but they too rebelled and were also dragged away into captivity by the nation of Babylon. During this period God sent prophets to warn and implore both Israel and Judah to turn back to God. The Major Prophets were Isaiah, Jeremiah and Ezekiel. The prophet Daniel lived during the time of the Babylonian captivity. God also sent Minor Prophets to continue his warnings and calls to repent.

SOLOMON TO SLAVERY

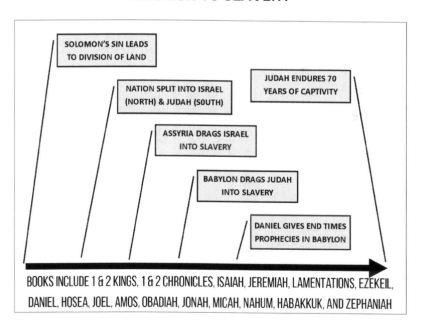

SOLOMON'S SIN LEADS TO DIVISION OF LAND

NATION SPLIT INTO ISRAEL (NORTH) & JUDAH (SOUTH)

JUDAH ENDURES 70 YEARS OF CAPTIVITY

ASSYRIA DRAGS ISRAEL INTO SLAVERY

BABYLON DRAGS JUDAH INTO SLAVERY

DANIEL GIVES END TIMES PROPHECIES IN BABYLON

BOOKS INCLUDE 1 & 2 KINGS, 1 & 2 CHRONICLES, ISAIAH, JEREMIAH, LAMENTATIONS, EZEKEIL, DANIEL, HOSEA, JOEL, AMOS, OBADIAH, JONAH, MICAH, NAHUM, HABAKKUK, AND ZEPHANIAH

▶ POST-CAPTIVITY TO THE REBUILDING OF JERUSALEM (INCLUDING SONGS AND POETRY)

This is the period of history where God used Esther to keep the Jewish people alive. And then the Prophet Nehemiah was used by God to help rebuild the wall around the city of Jerusalem so the Jews could come back to the land. Not only does Israel come back, but they experience a revival through the leading of Ezra. After this period was over, God remained silent for 400 years. God also left his people a rich library of songs, poetry, proverbs and epic stories.

POST-CAPTIVITY TO THE REBUILDING OF JERUSALEM (INCLUDING SONGS AND POETRY)

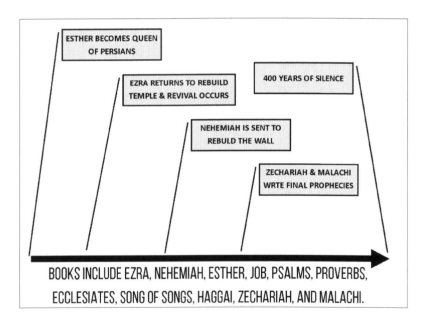

ESTHER BECOMES QUEEN OF PERSIANS

EZRA RETURNS TO REBUILD TEMPLE & REVIVAL OCCURS

400 YEARS OF SILENCE

NEHEMIAH IS SENT TO REBULD THE WALL

ZECHARIAH & MALACHI WRTE FINAL PROPHECIES

BOOKS INCLUDE EZRA, NEHEMIAH, ESTHER, JOB, PSALMS, PROVERBS, ECCLESIATES, SONG OF SONGS, HAGGAI, ZECHARIAH, AND MALACHI.

▶ THE LIFE OF CHRIST

This is the period of history where God's promised Son comes to earth to redeem mankind. Matthew, Mark, Luke and John were written by four of Jesus' followers telling the story of his life, death and resurrection. Known as the "Gospels" each of these books tells of the good news of Jesus' fulfillment of God's plan for mankind.

THE LIFE OF CHRIST

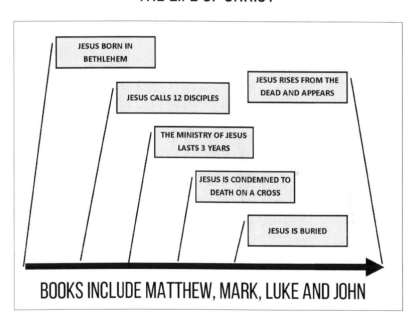

▶ THE CHURCH AGE

This is the period of history when the Son went to be with the Father and left the Holy Spirit to continue the Son's work on earth. This is considered the Apostolic Period when the

Disciples of Christ carried the Gospel around the world. This is also the time when Saul of Tarsus met Christ on the road to Damascus and was the chosen vessel to bring the Gospel to the Gentiles, later changing his name to Paul. Included in this period are the assorted letters to the different churches that were scattered around Asia and Europe. The main authors were Paul, Peter and John.

THE CHURCH AGE

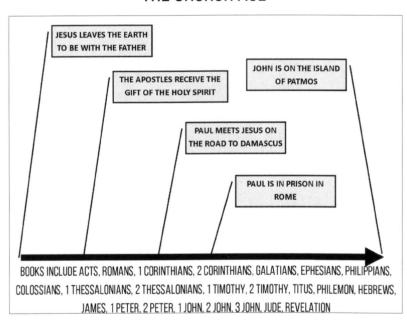

JESUS LEAVES THE EARTH TO BE WITH THE FATHER

THE APOSTLES RECEIVE THE GIFT OF THE HOLY SPIRIT

JOHN IS ON THE ISLAND OF PATMOS

PAUL MEETS JESUS ON THE ROAD TO DAMASCUS

PAUL IS IN PRISON IN ROME

BOOKS INCLUDE ACTS, ROMANS, 1 CORINTHIANS, 2 CORINTHIANS, GALATIANS, EPHESIANS, PHILIPPIANS, COLOSSIANS, 1 THESSALONIANS, 2 THESSALONIANS, 1 TIMOTHY, 2 TIMOTHY, TITUS, PHILEMON, HEBREWS, JAMES, 1 PETER, 2 PETER, 1 JOHN, 2 JOHN, 3 JOHN, JUDE, REVELATION

THE SCARLET THREAD

THE PURPOSE OF BIBLICAL HISTORY

After following all the charts, learning about all the books and reading the wide variety of verses you may wonder "Is there any way to boil it all down? Specifically, what is all of it about?" It seems to cover a lot of ground, how can anyone make sense of it all? After Jesus rose from the dead, he was talking to two men on the road to the city of Emmaus. They did not recognize him and they started talking to him about the events of the cross; nor did they quite understand why Jesus had to die. Jesus gives one of the most incisive answers found in scripture describing the purpose of scripture. Luke 24:44-48, put into your own words what he said:

_____

_____

_____

_____

_____

_____

Many people call this the "Scarlet Thread", all through scripture there are promises and prophesies that point to the coming of Christ and his subsequent death and resurrection. I will list the more famous verses that lead directly to Jesus.

1. GENESIS 3:15

In the first book of the Bible way back in the Garden of Eden, Adam and Eve were tempted by the Devil to sin against God. After they sinned God cursed both Adam and Eve and the Devil. In Genesis 3:15, God slips in a promise as he is cursing the Devil. What does it say?

How do you think this pertains to life of Christ?

How do the following New Testament verses help answer the previous question: Romans 16:20 & Hebrews 2:14:

2. GENESIS 12:1-3

When God called Abraham to be the "Father of Faith" he promised him that he would bless him, and the world through his offspring. How do you think this relates to Christ?

How do the following New Testament verses help answer the previous question: Acts 3:25 & Galatians 3:16:

3. GENESIS 49:8-10

When Jacob the Patriarch was about to die he gathered his 12 sons around him to give them a final prophecy and blessing. When he spoke to Judah he gave two very specific blessings. Write them down and write how you think they pertain to Jesus?

Jesus came from the lineage of Judah, and the promises given to Judah were to flow to him. How do the following New Testament verses show that he did receive Jacob's blessing: Philippians 2:5-11 & Revelation 5:5:

4. LEVITICUS 1:3-4

The book of Leviticus describes the religious laws when it comes to the sacrificial system. Leviticus 1:3-4 describes the kind of sacrifice that is acceptable to him. What does it say?

How do you think this relates to Christ?

How do the following New Testament verses help answer the previous question: John 1:29 & 1 Peter 1:19:

5. NUMBERS 24:17

In the book of Numbers, there was a prophet named Balaam. He was able to foresee future events and in Numbers 24:17 what did sign did he see from God?

How do you think that relates to Jesus?

_____

_____

_____

How does Matthew 2:2 & Revelation 22:16 bring clarity to the previous question?

_____

_____

_____

_____

6. DEUTERONOMY 32:39-43

This is a strange verse. Before Moses dies he gives a prophecy about how God himself will rescue his people by rendering vengeance on his enemies. It is a pretty gruesome. Describe what is going to happen in your own words:

_____

_____

_____

_____

How do you think this relates to Jesus?

_____

_____

_____

_____

How does 2 Thessalonians 1:6-11 & Revelation 19:11-21 helps answer the previous question?

_____

_____

_____

_____

7. 2 SAMUEL 7:12-16

King David served God faithfully, and as a result God gave to him one of the greatest promises in all of the Bible which is found in 2 Samuel 7:12-16. What does it say?

_____

_____

_____

_____

How do you think this relates to Jesus?

_____

_____

_____

How do the following verses in the New Testament help answer the previous question: Matthew 22:41-45, Hebrews 1:13, Romans 1:3 & 1 Corinthians 15:25-28:

_____

_____

_____

_____

8. ISAIAH 52:13-53:12

Isaiah had more prophecies about Jesus than any other prophet. In chapters 52 and 53 Isaiah makes some astounding prophecies about a servant of God that is going to come and suffer for the sins of many. Read it and write down things you know about Jesus that relate to what you just read:

_____

_____

_____

_____

How was this passage used in the book of Acts 8:26-40?

_____

_____

_____

_____

9. JEREMIAH 23:5-6

Jeremiah made an incredible prediction about a king that was coming. How did he describe him in Jeremiah 23:5-6?

_____

_____

_____

_____

How do you think this passage relates to Jesus?

_____

_____

_____

How do the following New Testament verses confirm what Jeremiah predicted: Luke 1:32 & Romans 10:4?

_____

_____

_____

10. MICAH 5:2

I want to offer you one more very specific prophecy. Read Micah 5:2 and put in to your own words what was he specific about.

_____

_____

_____

_____

How do you think that relates to Jesus?

_____

_____

_____

_____

What does Matthew 2:3-8 say about this?

_____

_____

_____

_____

What you just explored where only 10 verses that predicted some very specifics about Jesus and his coming. According to Isaiah 46:10-11, why are prophecies so important?

_____

_____

_____

_____

Do you know of any other leader, religious figure or person who had so many predictions made about him that came true?

_____

_____

_____

Jesus is the reason the Bible was written. So you could know him. See John 20:30:

_____

_____

_____

_____

CONSIDER A ROSE
A Final Thought on Purpose

A small red rose speaks volumes. It is understood by both the giver and receiver to be a vivid token of love.

A symbol of affection encased in a fragrant package of petals, stem and thorns. It is exquisite in its simplicity.

A rose when received, beholds both the visible beauty of the gift and unspoken intention of the giver. Lovers see in the red blossom the passion of the one whom they love. After the gift is received it must be put it on display: Maybe using a white, porcelain, long-stemmed vase or a simple glass cup. A lover's joy places the beauty of the gift somewhere prominent, a mantle, and table or bathroom countertop. A standing reminder of another's love.

Does more need to be done for the gift to be truly received? Do you need to know more about the gift for its beauty to be fully apprehended? Do you dissect the blossom to see if it has a stigma, style, anther and filament? Do you research what genus of rose, analyzing the prickle size and density of the stem? Is it necessary to know where it comes from, how it has been bred?

Or is it enough to simply receive it?

I have been in a discussion with a friend who recently asked me, "When it comes to salvation and God's word what must a person believe to fully receive it? What does someone "HAVE TO" believe in order to be considered a brother or sister in Christ? "

I find the answer to this question is more like receiving a gift than it is dissecting a plant. Like the rose, a person only needs to behold the beauty of the gift and see the intention of the giver through the gift.

Salvation is an exchange of love between two parties — it is not a thing to dissect. After salvation, you will want to display the gift, show others, and learn more and more about the gift you now possess. But like a rose, the gift can be completely received before the fullness of what it entails is understood.

When it comes to salvation, what is the gift and how do you behold its beauty? Scripture makes it very plain:

"But to all who did receive him (Jesus), those who believed in his name, he gave the right to become children of God, who were born, not of blood nor of the will of the flesh nor of the will of man, but of God."(John 1:12-13)

"And as Moses lifted up the serpent in the wilderness, so must the Son of Man be lifted up, that whoever believes in him may have eternal life." (John 3:14)

"Truly, truly, I say to you, whoever hears my word and believes him who sent me has eternal life. He does not come into judgment, but has passed from death to life." (John 5:24)

"I write these things to you who believe in the name of the Son of God, that you may know that you have eternal life." (1 John 5:13)

The Son is the gift, God is the giver of the gift, and all who truly love the Giver will receive the gift. What more needs to be known for the gift to be truly received? Only that the Son has been sent to you as a gift, albeit a necessary gift, from the Father out of love. Faith is the response of love on your part; faith is how a person fully and freely receives the gift.

If you try to pay the Giver for the gift, then it is no gift at all. And worse than that, when you think the love that you have been given has to somehow be earned, then that means you actually doubt both the character and intention of the Giver. And that is not a relationship based on love, but fear. Faith in the Son receives the gift fully. Sounds almost too simple?

There are many who see the Son, understand why he came, but they see no beauty in him. To him, he is not an expression of love from the Father, but a nuisance. This is a heart that has no faith. Demons believe and tremble. They know who the Son is but they don't love the Son, so they refuse him. Others, like the stubborn Pharisee, see the Son as someone to analyze, and with folded arms and wrinkled brow, demand for him to perform. If he satisfies their wishes they then may decide to pay for his services with a dutiful bend of the knee — paying for another's love is called prostitution. And God is no whore. He can't be bought; because love can't be bought.

Other Pharisees theologically dissect the Son. They don't see the Father's beauty in him as much as they see an object to scrutinize, to judge and lord over. A critical heart has no room for love:

"How can you say you are equal to the Father?"

"He has a demon, he is insane, why listen to him?"

"If you are the Son of God, come down off of that cross and save yourself?"

The Son was not seen as a gift but an unwanted invader. Those who are critics often master theology and are experts at the law, but they miss the beauty of the gift. "The god of this world has blinded the minds of the unbelievers, to keep them from seeing the light of the gospel of the glory of Christ, who is the image of God." (2 Cor. 4:4) In their blindness, they are emotionally stubborn, hard-hearted, and enemies to the giver of the gift.

Those who receive the gift welcome the Son with gladness. And when they welcome him, he comes to set up a home in their heart. Then, and only then, will they finally begin to see, understand and appreciate the fullness of who the Christ is, what the atonement means, and how the Trinity is sovereign over all the affairs of men. Then and only then will they start to love and understand his word.

"But the anointing that you received from him abides in you, and you have no need that anyone should teach you. But as his anointing teaches you about everything, and is true, and is no lie—just as it has taught you, abide in him." (1 John 2:27)

True understanding of the gift is a result of abiding with the Son. Until you receive him, you won't really know him. The heart must first be awakened by love, resulting in active faith, embracing the Son as your own. Faith in the Son receives the gift fully, completely, utterly. Like a rose, the beauty and fragrance of the Son draws me in and causes me to trust the heart of the Father. As Paul said in Acts 16:31. . .

"Believe on the Lord Jesus Christ, and you will be saved."

❖ If you need additional help understanding Salvation, we recommend the first booklet in this series, New Believers: A Four-Week Study Guide, which can also be purchased at:

www.christopherjweeks.com

ALSO AVAILABLE

Made in the USA
Coppell, TX
21 May 2021

55863996R20048